CHRISTIAN WITH BIPOLAR DISORDER

CHRISTIAN WITH
BIPOLAR DISORDER

DONNY WEIMAR

TATE PUBLISHING
AND ENTERPRISES, LLC

Published by Tate Publishing & Enterprises, LLC
127 E. Trade Center Terrace | Mustang, Oklahoma 73064 USA
1.888.361.9473 | www.tatepublishing.com

Tate Publishing is committed to excellence in the publishing industry. The company reflects the philosophy established by the founders, based on Psalm 68:11,
"The Lord gave the word and great was the company of those who published it."

Book design copyright © 2012 by Tate Publishing, LLC. All rights reserved.

Cover design by Joel Uber
Interior design by Chelsea Womble

Published in the United States of America

ISBN: 978-1-62024-661-0
Psychology / Psychopathology / Bipolar Disorder
12.06.27

ACKNOWLEDGMENTS

Thanks to my wife Eilene, my mother in law Nancy Kocur and brother in law Chris Kocur for encouragement, positive criticism, and exhortation in the writing of this first work.

Gratitude is extended to the Lord's church for which I labor with love.

All glory and praise to the High Priest who saves our souls.

Samuel is a fictitious character. He is a conglomeration of many people I have befriended over the years. He is similar to myself in many but not in all ways.

CONTENTS

CHRISTIAN WITH BIPOLAR DISORDER

By Donny Weimar

Samuel enters a locked chamber. Many questions probe his mind. The most dominant is the one he asks himself, "Why God?"

They lead him through the psychiatric observation room. At the end of a long row of recliners are two desks. After his vital signs are taken, he is seated at the side of the desk on the right. Samuel is told to remove everything from his pockets, his belt, his hoody jacket, and his shoes. An orderly rifles through his possessions, taking stock of every item in his wallet and the other things he had placed upon the desk. He diligently writes on a log sheet, which Samuel is told to sign before the contraband contents are sealed in a strong envelope.

Walking across the cold tile floor, he is escorted to the bathroom where he gives a urine sample. Then, he is asked to strip off all his clothing. They examine every inch of his body for injuries, scars, tattoos or track marks. Allowed to half redress, he is issued hospital socks and taken to the emergency observation room.

Samuel reclines in the fourth from the right. There are three long rows of chairs in what he is told is the Green Oaks Hospital psychiatric emergency room. Between his legs there is placed a sack lunch, which at three o'clock in the morning he welcomes as a blessing from God. This will be his third of seven hospitalizations.

As a Christian, Samuel understands Paul's thorn. The apostle writes in 2 Corinthians 12:7 *"And lest I should be exalted above measure by the abundance of the revelations, a thorn in the flesh was given to me, a messenger of Satan to buffet me, lest I be exalted above measure."* Some scholars believe Paul is going blind. Whatever it is, this champion evangelist is stricken with a disease God will not cure. Paul goes on to proclaim the Good News of Jesus for the remainder of his life.

No matter what the Devil afflicts us with, whether it is bipolar disorder, schizophrenia, or some other disease of the mind, Christians suffering with mental illness will not stop living for the Lord. We will remain committed to Jesus who has redeemed us from our iniquities. As is commonly heard by those successfully recovering from a mental illness, "I have bipolar disorder, but bipolar disorder does not define me." Though agonizing, Samuel can continue to be who he is – he just has a *thorn*. Jesus says that all who are heavily burdened can come to Him for rest (Matthew 11:28-30). Such should be the attitude of a Christian with mental illness.

I.

EMOTIONS –
GOD CREATED THEM

We are created in the image of God. Like our Creator, we possess a storehouse of emotions, as all people do. Tears of sadness pour down Jesus' cheeks (John 11:35); the Ephesians are told to *"be angry and, do not sin"* (Eph. 4:26). Psalm after Psalm recite the joy of serving Jehovah. Fear. Jealousy. Wrath. Rejoicing. Peace. Humility. Happiness. Every emotion we may possess is found in the Bible.

Christians, however, are not told in the New Testament we will be temporally happy. The sublime comes when we reach Paradise. In the ancients, the majority of Christians suffer with one affliction or another. Jesus is crucified with nails piercing his hands and feet. It is said that the apostle Peter is crucified upside down. Much of the brotherhood is thrown into prison, raped, torn in two or some other cowardly act of Jews and Romans. Of that time it is written, *"Yes, and all who desire to live godly in Christ Jesus will suffer persecution"* (2 Tim. 3:12). In 70 A.D., all saints (Christians) suffer.

Emotions are not sinful. If God designs us to have them, they are inherently good. It is not emotions in and of themselves that God wills we erase, but rather what we do with those feelings. We must learn to exercise self-control and temperance in all things. In all our feelings, God's children must submit to the Lord of our life (James 4:7).

Temptations are primarily governed by our emotions. The Spirit explains, *"But each one is tempted when he is drawn away by his own desires and enticed. Then, when desire has conceived, it gives birth to sin; and sin, when it is full-grown, brings forth death"* (Jas. 1:14-15). The Sly Serpent uses our own desires against us. Harness emotions, therefore; gain greater control of our failings.

Christians living with a mental illness may lead wholesome spiritual lives. They can yield the greater fruit (John 15:1-8). They can master their minds and be like Christ (Philippians 2:5). Mental illness is not a spiritual disease. It is not demon possession. And, it is controllable. By yielding ourselves to conformity with God's will we can become the strongest of the greatest strength. The Spirit inspires, *"do not be conformed to this world, but be transformed by the renewing of your mind, that you may prove what is that good and acceptable and perfect will of God"* (Rom. 12:2). To *renew* is to make a complete change for the better. All God's children have this task to undertake, daily. Mentally ill Christians are no different.

It may take six or even more hospitalizations before we finally are brought to our knees. Some stop taking their medications. Others are tormented with a major stressor. Sometimes medications simply stop working. In whatever scenario we face it; we must choose to press on to the higher calling of God. We must decide to do whatever it takes to get to Paradise. *"God has chosen the weak things of the world to put to shame the things which are mighty"* (1 Co. 1:27). We are weak, but our Lord is strong (Ephesians 6:10). Proverbs 14:26 presents the wisdom of King Solomon, *"In the fear of the LORD there is strong confidence, And His children will have a place of refuge.*

Emotions may also be biblically rewarding. To *bless*, means to make happy. Jesus spoke a lot about God's blessings. His beatitudes in Matthew 5:1-12 are a prime example. The suffering Christian may even rejoice during pain (Matthew 5:12). When glory is brought to God by our godly conduct, spiritual joy is the result. I tell you the truth; God wants to bless you!

So encourag- ing!

II.

UNDERSTANDING
BIPOLAR DISORDER

Bipolar Disorder is a disease. Also called manic-depressive illness, the disorder strikes more that two million adult Americans in any given year (National Institute of Mental Health – http://www.nimh.nih. gov). A brain condition, it causes a person's moods to shift from extreme highs (mania) to bottom lows (depression). With these mood swings, the afflicted person's energy rises and falls. Biological in its origins, bipolar disorder may erode rational thought and give rise to more strenuous temptations to do wrong.

Symptoms include but are not inherently limited to the following, as presented by the National Institute of Mental Health in a pamphlet entitled, "Bipolar Disorder," January 2007).

Signs and symptoms of mania (or a manic episode) include:

- Increased energy, activity, and restlessness

- Excessively "high," overly good, euphoric mood

- Extreme irritability

- Racing thoughts and talking very fast, jumping from one idea to another

- Distractibility, can't concentrate well

- Little sleep needed

- Unrealistic beliefs in one's abilities and powers

- Poor judgment

- Spending sprees

- A lasting period of behavior that is different from usual

- Increased sexual drive

- Abuse of drugs, particularly cocaine, alcohol and sleeping medications

- Provocative, intrusive, or aggressive behavior

- Denial that anything is wrong

Signs and symptoms of depression (or a depressive episode):

- Lasting sad, anxious, or empty mood

- Feelings of hopelessness or pessimism

- Feelings of guilt, worthlessness, or helplessness

- Loss of interest or pleasure in activities once enjoyed, including sex

- Decreased energy, a feeling of fatigue or of being "slowed down"

- Difficulty concentrating, remembering, making decisions

- Restlessness or irritability

- Sleeping too much, or can't sleep

- Change in appetite and/or unintended weight loss or gain

- Chronic pain or other persistent bodily symptoms that are not cause by physical illness or injury

- Thoughts of death or suicide, or suicide attempts

All of these symptoms do not have to co-exist for a diagnosis of Bipolar. Most literature seems to indicate the key number for mania is at least three symptoms for a duration of one week or longer. Depression is five or more for duration of at least two weeks. Self-diagnosis is dangerous and this book is only written for the purposes of educating and edifying the hurting. If you feel you or a loved one may have manic-depressive illness, seek professional guidance from a (preferably) Christian doctor.

III.

THE BIPOLAR BRAIN

God creates the brain. Like any other organ of the human body, it can become ill. The entire biology of the brain is too complex for the scope of this book. Nevertheless, a basic understanding of what happens in the brain when bipolar disorder occurs will ensure greater insight into one's condition.

The brain communicates within itself and the body chemically. Gray matter contains various types of cells, in particular to our understanding are the *neurons*. White matter holds the nerve's *axons*, which run between the neurons. Neurons reciprocate with one another electrochemically. Chemicals are created and travel down the length of the axon and released. These released chemicals are called *neurotransmitters*. The neurotransmitters fly through the *synaptic cleft*, which is the space between nerve cells, to the receptor cell. This reciprocal communication tells cells what to do. Containing literally billions of neurons, it is truly amazing they know which cells to communicate with and at the proper timing.

There are three neurotransmitter chemicals that concern bipolar illness: *Serotonin, Norepinephrine, and Dopamine.* It is believed when the level of these chemicals is too high, mania results and conversely when they are too low depression occurs. Mood stabilizing medications work to balance the levels of these neurotransmitters in the brain.

No concrete evidence can be found in the Bible as to why there are illnesses in the world. We can surmise that they have existed since Adam sinned, and therefore was ascribed a length of days. We may suspect that Satan afflicts us with various diseases, as did his devils in the Gospel Accounts. We do know for certain that God is the healer of body and spirit (Psalm 103:3). That He operates through the medical sciences is evidentiary.

Manic-depressive illness is as much a disease as is diabetes, heart disease, or cancer. It is treatable, though not yet curable. People suffering with bipolar must take medication and remain on a treatment plan for the remainder of their life. Balance is achievable. Thousands live a productive, normal life.

IV.

GOD'S PHYSICAL TREATMENTS

As with all biological illnesses, the right treatment plan must be implemented for healing to take place. In the next section of the book, we will delve into God's spiritual treatments for bipolar disorder. In this present section, we will present those things most commonly needed in an effective biological model.

The Right Hospitals

Many patients are not diagnosed properly until they are hospitalized. Sometimes, however, it takes more than one hospitalization to diagnose bipolar disorder. The illness can be elusive to doctors for the simple reason that most people don't seek help when they feel good, manic. They seek help when they are depressed, perhaps even suicidal. Police are sometimes dispatched and take the patient to the local emergency room where they are initially assessed. If a psychiatric disturbance is detected, they are then transferred to a psychiatric hospital.

There are two types of psychiatric hospitals, long term and short. Initial assessments are made at short-term psychiatric hospitals, which generally operate on the terms of the patient's insurance plan. Most hospital stays last no more than two weeks, and that is for medication adjustments and observation. Long-term facilities are usually state hospitals and house the worst cases. I am inclined to think that if you are reading this book, you do not fit into that description.

Voluntary registration at a private hospital usually places the limited control of how long a stay a patient desires. There are generally some terms that must be agreed upon between the hospital and the patient. One hospital for example, requires 24-hour notification so that the psychiatrist can examine the patient. If the patient is still too ill to be released, the request will be denied. It is in the patient's better interest.

Once the patient initially arrives at the hospital and all necessary paperwork has been filled out, he is usually seen by a general practitioner doctor for a physical examination. In some cases, an MRI may be ordered to rule out head injuries. Blood work is drawn by an experienced technician to test for various things relative to physical maladies, such as a thyroid condition.

Most psychiatric hospitals are immaculate. Televisions are located in sitting areas. They usually have their own gymnasiums and arts and crafts room. The bedroom is small and unless insurance pays for a private room, it is likely that the patient will not be alone. Personal items are limited and a list of allowed belongings should be obtained prior to registration.

Hospitalization is not fun. It is therapeutic and nothing more. Seldom is a patient found who wants a lengthy stay. The goal is to be properly diagnosed, medicated appropriately and counseled sufficiently.

The Right Physicians

The primary differences between a *psychologist* and a *psychiatrist* are that the former is more inclined to conduct a form of talk therapy (probably CBT) and the psychiatrist will follow the medical model. Both are capable of making diagnoses, but only the psychiatrist, as a medical doctor, is licensed to prescribe medication. Psychiatrists are licensed medical doctors with specialized training in the mental health field. He or she will interview the patient with gifted questioning and assessment. There is no medical test available to diagnose bipolar disorder. What there is is a manual called the *Diagnostic and Statistical Manual of Mental Disorders, Fourth Edition, Text-Revised*

(DSM-IV-TR). This book is the standard diagnostic manual for the mental health profession in the United States. Good psychiatrists know the manual like the back of their hand and are talented at making a sound diagnosis on the first or second visit, They base their analysis on what they hear and see in the assessment. If the client presents himself as depressed but gives no case history of mania, a misdiagnosis may occur. It is imperative that one be honest from the beginning.

The Right Medications

There are several medications used to treat manic-depressive illness. Mood stabilizers, antidepressants, anxiety meds, anti-psychotics, and a plethora of other medications may be used to treat the disease. Working with the doctor to find the right combination of medicines can sometimes be arduous. Don't allow frustration to sink in. There may be a period of trial and error. As time goes by mood balance will come. For some individuals medications will have to be adjusted as history rolls by. This may for some even require additional hospitalizations for observation while medications are updated and brought into harmony with current brain chemistry. This should be accepted as a part of having the disorder.

The most important thing for the bipolar person is to (*stay*) on the medications. For some, once a person begins to feel better he stops taking his meds and consequently relapses. This usually results in another hospitalization. When a person with bipolar is feeling *normal* it simply means the medicine is working as it should – don't stop taking it. I can't emphasize this enough. Sincere forgetting to take medicine is also a problem. It is important to maintain the correct level of medicines in the system, especially with such medications as Lithium. Pillboxes with days and times labeled on them may be inexpensively purchased at practically any pharmacy. If a loved one or partner is willing to remind the person of med time, this will also go a long way toward healthy medication management. Some people also purchase watches with alarms on them; set them to go off at the next scheduled time for taking meds.

The Right Therapists

While psychiatrists handle the biology of brain chemistry with psychotropic medicine, therapists are equipped to help the client *cope* with the condition and other life issues impacted by the disease. Filling this role may be psychiatric social workers, licensed professional counselors and psychologists.

In therapy, unearthing *triggers* is to be an early task. Triggers are life stressors that cause episodes of mania or depression to begin. Stress, whether created in a worrisome mind or major life changes are the most common triggers. After a while, early detection of manic or hypomanic episodes can be identified as quickly as depression.

Learning to deal with anxiety, grief, anger, low self-esteem, and other emotional issues commonly faced by those suffering with bipolar disorder are handled in sessions with the qualified therapist. Session lengths are generally no more than an hour and can be as frequent as twice a week, in the beginning of work.

The qualified therapist will have proper credentials. A minimum of a master's degree; psychiatric experience with mood disorders; state licensure, and as far as this author is concerned, a Christian background. Having a Christian background, however, does not inherently equip her to be your therapist. Some believe in demonology and not the biological roots of mental illness. Such is a deception of clear scientific and biblical evidence.

The therapeutic model that best fits the biblical approach to counseling those with bipolar disorder is called *Cognitive Behavioral Therapy* (CBT). CBT works through the power of logic and positive reinforcement. Using the right questions and coaching

AND God!

CHRISTIAN WITH BIPOLAR DISORDER

the therapist probes for *irrational thoughts and beliefs* then helps the client correct their faulty reasoning, which leads to emotional problems. As perspectives change and behaviors are modified the client becomes better equipped to live with the bipolar illness.

V.

GOD'S SPIRITUAL TREATMENTS

God is more powerful than Satan. God has always limited the Devil as to how far and how much he may go in afflicting us with disease, pestilence, war, famine and the like. Take Job for instance. *"And the LORD said to Satan, 'Behold, all that he has is in your power; only do not lay your hand on his person'"* (Job 1:12). The Devil murders Job's sons, wipes out his finances and strikes him with *"painful boils from the sole of his foot to the crown of his head"* (2:7). It is so fierce that Job's wife exclaims to him, *"Do you still hold fast to your integrity? Curse God and die!"* (2:9). He's even lost his support system. Friends approach Job to attempt to comfort him. They offer possible reasons for why he is plagued. The most popular is that some sin he has committed has brought God's curse upon him. Job held to his integrity. In all that occurs, *"Job did not sin nor charge God with wrong"* (1:22). Being diagnosed with bipolar disorder is not your fault. You did not do something to bring the disease upon yourself. That is largely genetics. As for Job, when his trial is over the *"Lord restored Job's losses when he prayed for his friends. Indeed the Lord gave Job twice as much as he had before"* (Job 42:10). Christians living with bipolar strive to receive the ultimate Prize.

We must accept the biblical truth that it is Satan who afflicts us with disease and every evil thing that occurs on the earth (1 Peter 5:8-9). God is on our side. He takes *the lemons life hands us and turns them into lemonade.* All things work together for good to them that love the Lord (Romans 8:28).

What God is most concerned with is our soul. The body comes second. For the soul to be healthy, however, the body too must be treated, as it is the vessel of our living spirit. The Lord works through the medical fields to heal our body of various maladies. He uses the Bible and Holy Spirit to touch our soul (Ephesians 6:17). What are presented here are biblical insights into living with manic-depressive illness: how to combat temptations; cope with mania and depression; and win the war against Satan and his allies. We will find grace to help in time of need.

Remember, all people experience mood swings. The difference for the disorder is that those moods and swings are extremely inflated. As they exaggerate, Satan pulls the right strings to tempt us into doing things we would not normally do and think things we would not normally think. Sinners have no control over their indulgences because they are already enslaved to sin (John 8:34). When we became Christians by the grace of God we gained power over sinning and it is now unnatural for us (Romans 8).

We accept forgiveness and embrace self-control. Temptations are common to everyone. One does not have to be diagnosed with bipolar disorder to acquire a drug addiction, commit sexual immorality, strive in quarrels, malice, be a poor steward, steal, waste money, gamble, or any other reckless behavior. Having the disease, however, may make one more inclined to do such things. The sickness is unlikely to be miraculously cured. So, we must all do our best to overcome the evils and embrace the gifts.

VI.

BIBLICAL COPING SKILLS
FOR MANIA

It sneaks up on us like lightening in the sky. Fiercely striking euphoria from hell. It ignites our hearts with feel good passions and lusts of the flesh; mania is the peak of bipolar disorder. As it grows from normalcy to impassionate zest, we travel up the road with the pedal on the floor. Faster and faster we go. Our thoughts race. Our speech won't move fast enough so it sounds pressed and stuttered. On and on we climb. We feel emblazoned with sex and enamored with spending. Up. Up. We climb. We become someone great and powerful. We acquire the ability to win friends and influence people. We are the smartest, sexiest, bravest, noblest, kindest, best-est person alive! This feels so-o-o-o-o freakin' good! Don't mess with us. We will rip you to pieces with our words or fist. We will tear you limb by limb until you are squashed beneath our feet.

You peon, how dare you mess with us!?! This world belongs to us! Crash.

For most people, mania feels good. God wants us to feel good, but He does not want us to be unhealthy. Euphoria escalates us into higher temptations that the Devil uses to make war against us. Christians are at constant battle with temptations of the mind and flesh. With bipolar disorder emotions are inflated, lending more power to the sway of evil. Equipping self with biblical coping skills and tools to cast down the Sly Serpent, we are better able to conquer sinning.

Euphoric explorations open the spirit to all sorts of manifestations. Manic symptoms, however, are often difficult to self-identify and denial is powerful. We must learn to trust and accept the judgment of the Holy Spirit, professionals and loved ones.

Unlike Cain in the Bible, we accept that we are our brother's keeper, and they ours. Christians pray for one another and catch us when we stumble. At least one trusted friend should know about our condition. Having someone to interact with on a regular basis that knows our strengths and weaknesses allows for Christian intervention when we fail ourselves. It provides a prayer partner and someone to turn to when we fall short of glorifying God.

Privacy is a big issue. If you don't want the proverbial cat out of the bag, don't share with a gossip. There are laws, which prevent health and insurance

CHRISTIAN WITH BIPOLAR DISORDER

companies from divulging private health information. Some Christians, however, blab everything we tell them. Gossip is as much a sin as any other. We must have confidence.

The following points highlight some of the greater weaknesses of manic Christians. They are not a list of the total picture and these are touched on only to enhance our abilities to combat spiritual warfare. God is on our side.

> *In all these things we are more than conquerors through Him who loved us.*
>
> Romans 8:37

Controlling Poor Judgment

Mania takes upon itself an impulsive nature that often reflects with poor judgment. It clouds one's thinking. Since Christianity is largely the religion of the mind, as it is said to be our *reasonable* (logical) service (Romans 12:1), we must store as much Scriptural knowledge and wisdom in our minds as we may get there. There are three biblical recommendations for *preparing* for a period of poor judgment, all dealing with wisdom. First, pray for wisdom (James 1:5-7). As found in this passage, wisdom is not mere common sense. Common sense as we call it deals more with earthly wisdom, making daily decisions in life affairs. The Bible is mainly concerned with morality, doing that which pleases the Lord. Thus, the wisdom to be found in James 1 is *spiritual insight into living in a carnal world*. It helps us to cut through the fog, with the insightful lights of Divine wisdom. With every temptation common to man, God shows an escape (1 Corinthians 10:13). Wisdom from above helps enable us to find that escape.

Second, study the book of Proverbs. The twentieth book of the Bible, the Proverbs of Solomon and other Spirit filled men write from the perspective of a father instructing his son on the ways of life. Much common sense, earthly wisdom, is unearthed here and a lot is devoted to keeping oneself pure. It is in this book that we learn, *"The fear of the LORD is the beginning of knowledge, But fools despise wisdom and instruction"* (Pr. 1:7).

Third, read the Gospel Accounts (Matthew, Mark, Luke and John). It says of young Jesus, *"the Child grew and became strong in spirit, filled with wisdom; and the grace of God was upon Him"* (Luke 2:40 emphasis mine). The word *Christian* itself means to be like, or a follower of, Christ. To study the Master gives us the mark for which we aim to emulate. We read in another place that Christ Jesus is both the power and wisdom of God (1 Corinthians 1:24). As such, the more we walk with the Master the more we become like Him. From Jesus, we learn to bear temptations. We listen to Him calm life's vehement storms. Streams of living water flow into us like a well springing up unto eternal life. Our judgment improves because we obtain the mind of Christ (1 Corinthians 2:16). We come to think, as He thinks. Jesus' attitude, logic and morality are funneled into our souls.

Irritability

To be easily annoyed or angered lends to a wrathful character. Anger itself is an emotion God gave us. It is not inherently sinful to be angry. What we do with the emotion will determine whether it's behaviors are sinful or righteous. God watches the actions, attitudes and motives. If a brother is angered by the sinful actions of his neighbor, he has a right to righteous indignation but must not sin with his words or actions. On the other hand if he is irritated by something that may be annoying but not sinful, he has no cause for expressing a wrathful spirit. Wrath is anger expressed in a form of punishment. It can be violent and abusive. Such violent anger is reserved for God alone in the Day of Judgment. Hence the Spirit's admonition, *"Be angry, and do not sin: do not let the sun go down on your wrath"* (Eph. 4:26).

Coping with an irritable disposition begins with prayer (1 Thessalonians 5:17). By giving our feelings over to the Lord we trust in His power to mend our disturbance. We allow God to take the helm of our heart. We lean on this principle: *"Beloved, do not avenge yourselves, but rather give place to wrath; for it is written, 'Vengeance is Mine, I will repay,' says the Lord"* (Rom. 12:19). Secondly, we draw upon our capacity to reason within ourselves. Our emotional mind must not have dominion over our rational. Forcing ourselves to think about our circumstances bring more sound judgment to surface. Third, realize that we cannot control the thoughts and actions of others. We can only control how we react to their actions. It is our own heart that must first be right with God. To be angry with somebody implies we have judged their actions or words to be contrary to our beliefs, attitudes, actions, motives and so forth. Jesus teaches us to *"first remove the plank from your own eye, and then you will see clearly to remove the speck from your brother's eye"* (Mat. 7:5).

Things don't always go our way. There has to be a little rain in our life for us to appreciate the sunshine. Life can be frustrating, angering and downright annoying. We lose health, money and relationships but we must not forfeit our faith. If we are in the routine of uncontrolled anger, seek professional counseling. Do whatever is necessary to become a generally happy person.

Increased Sex Drive

Heightened emotions may invite sexual immorality. Mania is the cause of many divorces on such Scriptural grounds as these (Matthew 19:9). Between people, sexual immorality is called by four names in the Bible: fornication, adultery, sodomy and homosexuality. Adultery is generally understood as a sexual violation of the marriage covenant (Matthew 5:32). Homosexuality is listed among other sins, including sodomy that will bar one from entering the Kingdom of God (1 Corinthians 6:9). It is sexual immorality between people of the same gender. Sodomy is biblically equivalent to pedophilia in today's terms. Fornication is a much more broad term, simply translated in most modern versions as sexual immorality. The most common form of sexual immorality encountered by Christians is pornography – lust, lasciviousness and sex in the mind.

God intends for sex to be between husband and wife, and they alone. Its design is for procreation but also bonds the couple into *one flesh*. All people face the temptation of fornication, but people living with bipolar commonly see a higher drive towards it during the manic episode.

Handling this temptation can begin with memorization of key Bible passages dealing with the temptation (cf. Colossians 3:5). Jesus defeated the Tempter three times in the wilderness by reciting Scripture (Matthew 4:1ff). The Bible is powerful. The sword of the Holy Spirit is the word of God (Ephesians 6:17). We are sanctified by God's word (John 17:17). The Scriptures contain protective properties for the saint. *"As for God, His way is perfect; The word of the LORD is proven; He is a shield to all who trust in Him"* (Psa. 18:30).

Second, run away. In Genesis 39 it is told that Potiphar's wife attempted to seduce Joseph. It is said, *"that she caught him by his garment, saying, 'Lie with me.' But he left his garment in her hand, and fled and ran outside"* (Gen. 39:12). No matter the accusations. Regardless of the consequences, we must *run* away from the seductress. Joseph is falsely accused of attempting to rape Potiphar's wife and is consequently thrown into prison. Better there than shackled in sin. As is it is written in 1 Corinthians 6:18 *"Flee sexual immorality. Every sin that a man does is outside the body, but he who commits sexual immorality sins against his own body."*

Third, as at all times pray. Pray that God will give us a stronger spiritual constitution than a physical attraction. Realize than inner purity is of greater virtue than outward beauty. Passions of the flesh are temporary and perish. Christ is forever.

Addictions

Jesus sets forth this axiom: *"No one can serve two masters; for either he will hate the one and love the other, or else he will be loyal to the one and despise the other. You cannot serve God and mammon"* (Mat. 6:24). Mammon is money. Principal the point applies to any kind of idolatry. An idol in modern philosophy is anything that we set up as a god in our life. If we become addicted to something, it masters us. We serve it. Christians only have one Master, Jesus Christ.

Drugs, alcoholism, caffeine, tobacco, and any other addictive substances are definite no-no's for God's children. In the New Testament, bishops must be sober to be qualified for their office. Sobriety in the ancients meant to have a sound mind and curbing one's desires. Addictions such as these inhibit the thought processes of the mind and alter perceptions. They influence attitudes and demonstrate a lack of mental stability.

Substance abuse requires systematic detoxification. With this penitent process, the Christian must trust the forbearance of God, as the addiction is defeated. There is a difference between tolerance and forbearance in the eyes of God. Tolerance puts up with sin with no view to bring the sinner to repentance. Forbearance tolerates sin for a season, while repentance works to restore the soul to the righteous path. There is a sense in which we are all under the constant forbearance of the Father. Our walk in the light is a constant turning away from sin and movement towards God.

Often substance abuse addictions begin with the innocent attempt to self medicate. They feel good. Either stimulating the brain to excitement or slowing the world down to feel more manageable degrees. Such indulgences can actually trigger and alter episodes, or render prescribed medications limp. It takes courage to admit an addiction and help to overcome. God works through the medical fields, social programs, group counseling and the convicting Holy Spirit to bring healing to the addicted saint.

Spending Sprees

"God is able to make all grace abound toward you, that you, always having all sufficiency in all things, may have an abundance for every good work" (2 Co. 9:8). God gives us money to share with those around us who are suffering hardships. We labor with our hands to earn this gift. For this reason, stealing is a sin (Ephesians 4:28). There is another word in the Bible dealing with money going directly to the heart of the issue of spending sprees.

Stewardship. Christians are financial managers. Every gift God places into our care is entrusted to us as a manager, or steward, of that gift. If we are faithful we will be blessed with more, and conversely less with poor stewardship. See Matthew 25:14 and read the parable of the talents to ponder this subject.

Uncontrolled spending sprees are poor stewardship. I know one Christian who spent $11,500.00 in one day on a spending spree. Another bought a $54,000 automobile with good credit and no employment. The dealership would not accept mental illness as good grounds for the car to be returned. We spend money like this because it feels good. But, remember feelings are deceptive.

Christians who spend when manic need a trustee to manage their money when they become ill. If married or have a close loved one, that person should be the steward of monetary interests. Credit cards are to be shredded. Banks can post daily and weekly spending limits on debit check cards. Very little allowance money should be kept in the purse or wallet.

The manic Christian finds grace to help in time of need (Hebrews 4:16). The physical malady has spiritual ramifications. Left uncontrolled, mania leads to a world of iniquity. There is help. A disease does not define where one will spend eternity. Between the help of trained medical workers, therapists and Christian loved ones, those living in a manic state can find remedies for their spiritual situation.

VII.

DEFLATING DEPRESSION WITH SPIRITUAL THINKING

*Yes, we had the sentence of death in ourselves, that
we should not trust in ourselves but in God who
raises the dead*

2 Corinthians 1:9

The crushing darkness weighs like the dead. Upon
our knees we pray for deliverance. The spell of tears
stream down our face and salt in the corners of our
mouth do nothing to soothe the sting in our eyes as
our sinuses swell. Guilt consumes us without cause.
We feel worthless and almost numb from the weeks
of sleep. Little food has entered our mouths as our
appetite diminishes with the anguish that increases
with each loathsome breath we take. Our clothes are
slept in. The deodorant that we put on last week has
long since stopped its effectiveness. A bird must have
made its nest in our hair.

Annoyed when disturbed, unfathomable words fly out of our mouths to innocent ones who we once hoped would not inherit our disease. The hobbies we once enjoyed are useless for relaxation. Reading is almost impossible as the concentration it requires drains what mental functioning we have.

Each day is a daunting task. We eat less and sleep more. We get to the point of exasperation where we feel life is simply too hard. Stop the pain. Give us feelings. We're foolish. We're sinners. We're unforgivable. There's no hope.

To the major depressed, the world is cold and dismal. In the darkness dwells the most painful of feelings. It is the state of crisis in which most people finally are brought to their knees desperate for help. Everything that goes up (mania) must come crashing down (depression). At the bottom of despair is the ugliness that can spell death. This is the time the doctor will see most bipolar clients. Downcast spirits of the afflicted soul have hope – from God.

Sadness

Depressed King David says in Psalm 116:3, *"The pains of death surrounded me, And the pangs of Sheol laid hold of me; I found trouble and sorrow."* His trust in God is monumental. This is a king who commits all manner of atrocities, yet he remains in the Lord's favor. During his reign he commits adultery with Bathsheba, plots the death of her husband and lies about his fraud. There are dire consequences to his actions. His firstborn son dies at the hand of God. David does not give up his salvation. And, that my friend is how we endure depression. We trust God.

There is always an end to depression. God does not allow us to suffer so long as to murder our soul. It is painful, yes. But, we do swing again. Normalcy is found. There is that proverbial *light at the end of the tunnel*. Once again, sin is not the cause of bipolar depression. Remember Job. It is Satan who has afflicted us with this terrible disease.

God enables us to hang on. *"For You delivered my soul from death, My eyes from tears"* (Psa. 116:8). Out of envy and rage King Saul hunts David down. He seeks to kill him before he can replace him on the throne. God guides David's steps. The King of kings leads us too. Through long days, past the irritability, beyond the highway of hell He leads us hand in hand. It is not at a funeral dirge that the king writes, *"Yea, though I walk through the valley of the shadow of death, I will fear no evil; For You are with me; Your rod and Your staff, they comfort me"* (Psa. 23:4).

A good friend of mine taught me to say into the mirror, *"I am too blessed to be depressed."* As we count our blessings, we begin to think more positively about the good in life. Whether it be a warm meal, the smile on our daughter's face, the laughter of good friends, a bed to lie in, the beauty of the sunset, or a hot cup of java. Think of it this way, if we never became depressed we would take for granted the good feeling of being happy.

We pray like kings seeking wisdom in the affairs of God's house. No matter how fierce the depression there is no logical reason to give up. In our low feelings we must do as the Master says, *"Then Jesus said to His disciples, "If anyone desires to come after Me, let him deny himself, and take up his cross, and follow Me"* (Mat. 16:24).

God has sent us a Comforter (Acts 9:31). That the apostles and evangelists write on several occasions to fellow Christians thanking them for their comfort implies periods of discouragement and quite possibly depression (2 Corinthians 7:13). We receive ease for our pain from God and from brethren. Suffering saints need one another. Of the most tempting things for the depressed person to do is to shut oneself up alone and slumber. All the while the two best things we can do in Scriptural principle is be with encouraging people and worship God.

To a world without Christ, King Solomon writes in Ecclesiastes 4:1 *"Then I returned and considered all the oppression that is done under the sun: And look! The tears of the oppressed, But they have no comforter -- On the side of their oppressors there is power, But they have no com-*

forter." To a church filled with the Holy Spirit, apostle Paul writes in 2 Corinthians 1:4 "[God] *comforts us in all our tribulation, that we may be able to comfort those who are in any trouble, with the comfort with which we ourselves are comforted by God."* Major Depression is the greatest emotional trouble that we may have ever known. In that distress, we have a God who comforts. That is to say no matter how deep into the darkness we fall, it is God who keeps us from hitting the deadly bottom. Not only that, the comfort He gives we may reciprocate to others suffering around us. The healthy thing for a suffering saint to do when downtrodden is to be of some help to somebody else. As the Hebrew writer puts it, *"Let us therefore come boldly to the throne of grace, that we may obtain mercy and find grace to help in time of need"* (4:16).

Feelings of Guilt

There is a real difference between true and false guilt, clinically. False guilt is arrived at by delusional thoughts, false or irrational beliefs. It assumes the role of making us feel we have done something wrong when in reality no transgression has transpired. Depression lends us to this trap. The Devil is sly. If he can deceive us into thinking we have wronged someone, something or God when we haven't, we will find ourselves in a place where forgiveness is difficult to be found – especially if the somebody we believe we've wronged is ourselves. True or false, healing may be found.

God sent His Son to redeem sinners. Redemption is to buy back; we were sold into the slavery of sin. Biblically, guilt occurs when the sting of sin pricks our hearts (cf. Acts 2:37). It causes sorrow. Of that sorrow there are two sorts. 2 Corinthians 7:10 states *"For godly sorrow produces repentance leading to salvation, not to be regretted; but the sorrow of the world produces death."* The emotion of godly sorrow dries up once repentance is processed. Again, repentance is a change of mind that produces a change of lifestyle. The penitent Christian has the constant aim to walk away from sin unto the Christ who saves to the uttermost. Now, here's the thing. Once God has forgiven us of some transgression, we're forgiven. Period. There is no cause to continue our remorse. We have turned unto to the God of grace and been healed in the soul.

One of the most difficult things for a Christian to do is to forgive self. We are intellectually aware that the precious blood of the Lamb washes our sins away; and that blood continues to purge our iniquities. But, we persist at nagging ourselves over things we should have done differently. This friend is doubt. The Devil does not want us to believe in grace. He wants us to wallow in the pigpen of selfish denial. Trust me, when

God says He will do something, He does it. Satan does not run the show. Thus, the message is *let go*.

Let go of the shame and embarrassment. Let go of the self pity and despair. Give it all to Jesus. He is the One who cares when we feel lonely, isolated and in want. Jesus is the Christ, the Son of the living God. When His grace touches our ill soul we find grace and mercy to help in our moment of need. Don't feel guilty. Just let go.

Low Self Esteem

Perhaps it is what we were taught as children. There is something wrong with mentally ill people. They are crazy, lunatics, weird. Or, maybe it was the way we were treated by adults growing up. Then again, could it have been the way we were different than the other children and frankly stayed to ourselves? No matter the history, the diagnosis changes us somehow. That too is fallacious thinking.

We have bipolar; we are not bipolar. Understand? The illness does not define who we are. God sees us as more important than the flowers in the field or the birds in the air (Matthew 6). So, don't worry. There is an old poster floating around out there somewhere that reads, "I know I'm somebody 'cause God don't make no junk!"

The entire scheme of redemption is for us. You and me. Of all the creation God makes, He sent His Son to save you! The earth and all the works done therein will be burned up on the Day of Judgment. He won't save the crickets, flowers, sun, stars or even the house we grew up in. Jesus miserably suffered, bled and died so that we may live life to its fullest potential. There is no time to sulk about all that we aren't. We must take the day, each day God blesses us with and appreciate it for all its glory.

I want you to think about something. All temptations are common to all people (1 Corinthians 10:13). But, for us they are inflated when we're manic. We overcome them just like everybody else. That makes us stronger than the average Christian. Why? Because we have to put more effort into it. Again, everybody gets depressed from time to time. But, major depression is more severe. We hang in there. We outlast the pain and suffering. That makes us stronger than the average person. We face the stigma. We endure tears longer.

Anxiety

Forty million Americans are affected by one of several kinds of Anxiety Disorders in any given year, according to the National Institute of Mental Health. Anxiety comorbid with Bipolar Disorder is not uncommon at all. Fear is at the core of all of the disorders. There are two basic genres of anxiety where this book concerns itself; worry and clinical anxiety. The former is sinful according to Scripture.

He says, *"do not worry..."* In Matthew 6:25-34 Jesus discusses the kind of anxiety that wars against the soul. The bottom line of His message is that there is no need for the disciple to be so obsessed with daily provisions as to fret over where they are going to come from. The following account demonstrates the battle.

Samuel is a veteran preacher of eighteen years. In December of 2007 he looses his third church due to having bipolar. The second church let him go after his second hospitalization. He had had a fight with his wife, gotten into his pickup and driven for miles and miles into the middle of nowhere. When he comes to a grocery store he phones home not knowing where he is or how he got there. His wife interrupts a church fellowship to ask one of the overseers to help get him home. The following Sunday he said he was ready to retake the pulpit. But, the church has lost trust in Samuel and the elders have no choice but to fire him. Some months go by and he and his family acquire a work 1,500 miles away in Delaware.

He doesn't tell the church he is bipolar in fear of losing that work too. The symptoms persist and he has a major depressed episode. Wanting help, he breaks down and tells the elders. Instead of getting help, he loses their trust. A year passes and the elders finally bring him into the office. One of them says he has no faith in Samuel. That he doesn't trust him. That cold September night, the day after his birthday the elders "let him go." They gave him time to relocate.

After sending several resumes and going on interviews, the ministry jobs just weren't coming. Just before Christmas on a blistering Wednesday night, the elders present a deadline. Samuel had to go.

He moves his family back to Texas, into his in-laws house. 2008 will prove a most difficult year. Samuel applies to so many churches and secular works that he loses count. He is living on dwindling family savings. His worry over daily provisions is surmounting. January through March are spent going from one small church to the next interviewing for ministries.

Samuel finally emails a church leader to ask why he didn't get the job. The reply comes back, "We observed mood swings in your preaching and behavior that disturbed us. We enjoyed your preaching but feel we must protect our congregation from unknown emotional problems you may have."

Refusing to give up, Samuel sends out another thirty resumes to churches all across the United States. None of them even respond. In May he finally lands a low-income job as a security guard. Part of the job is stressful requiring multi-tasking. Two months into the job, another depression episode is triggered that lands him in Timber Lawn Hospital.

Upon release his doctor issues a memo allowing him to go back to work on a set date. Ignorant of the secular work world, Samuel misses the date and is again fired. This will be the last full-time employment he will see for the year. Now there is no income, again. June, Samuel's wife begins substitute teaching in September and makes plans to earn her teaching certificate. But, how will we survive another year that the plan requires?

Samuel enters Glenn Oaks Hospital.

God takes care of Samuel's family. He provides a house to stay in. Pays all his utility bills. He gives him food stamps. The church with whom they are worshipping pays Samuel every time he fills in the pulpit. Two small churches of eleven and fifteen members hire Samuel to preach every Sunday. Individual Christians contribute collectively thousands of dollars over the course of the year. His family never misses a meal. His children's school uniforms are donated. Even the Christmas tree with lights included is given to his family.

The point. There is nothing to worry about. God takes care of His children. There are actually only two things the Lord promises faithful Christians in the material world. They are the same two things He gave Adam & Eve. He promises food and clothing –

that's it (Matthew 6:25, 33). God does not promise we won't be homeless. Jesus Himself had no place to lay his head (Matthew 8:20). God does not guarantee we will have employment, good health, an automobile, or even clean hair. The Christian, therefore is not overly concerned with earthly provisions. We concern ourselves with the Kingdom. As Jesus concludes, *"But seek first the kingdom of God and His righteousness, and all these things shall be added to you"* (Mat. 6:33).

Clinical anxiety is not mere worry. It is caused biologically and triggered primarily by stress. It too involves fear. The most common anxiety disorders are: Panic Disorder, Generalized Anxiety Disorder, Obsessive Compulsive Disorder, Post-Traumatic Stress Disorder, Social Anxiety Disorder, and other phobias. Writing on the biblical coping strategies on all of these disorders is beyond the scope of this book. Know this. There is help from doctors, medicines, therapists, and of course God.

Feeling Helpless

Where is God? Having tried several doctors and medications, been literally down on our face in prayer we may still feel desperate. We feel broken and there is nobody to repair us. We are good for nothing but to be thrown out with the rubbish. Or, so we think.

Never forget that God is on our side. Through the pain He sustains us. Delivered from all his enemies and the hands of the man who stalked to take his life, David says, *"The LORD is my rock and my fortress and my deliverer"* (2 Sa. 22:2). We are not alone in the fiery furnace. God's Angel stands there with us (Daniel 3:25). Because we are Christians, we have more help, more strength and more ability to cope than the millions who do not know the Lord of life.

We have the perfect High Priest who intercedes with the Father on our behalf (Hebrews 7). The Holy Spirit guides our heart to see that we are moving closer to God as we walk in the way of truth and righteousness. Fellow saints build us up and encourage us when we need them most. The Lord's church is a mighty fortress, a house of prayer. We have more going for us than against us. Now is not the time to feel helpless.

In fact, because we understand emotional crisis we are better equipped to minister to the needs of others like ourselves. We have become more empathetic, understanding the pain of mental illness. Because we suffer we understand more about the emotional turmoil Jesus surely endured. He took the weight of the world's sins on Himself as He humbly sacrificed Himself on the cross. He could have called thousands of angels to rescue Him, but He chose to suffer that we might have access to God's throne of grace. Since we better understand His emotional pain, we can become even more like Him than our counterparts who have only read about His agony. Helpless? Oh, no. Helpful.

Feeling Lonely

Sitting in the tenth pew from the front is a sister with bipolar disorder. The congregation of about two hundred souls is preparing for worship. The sister feels lonely. Not because nobody speaks to her, but because she feels very different from everybody else. She hasn't told a single person in the church about her condition, but she is certain her depressive emotions are transparent. (Most people actually cannot see what another person is truly feeling.) Because she hasn't said anything to her brothers and sisters in Christ she feels isolated, not feeling free to be herself. This is a choice and the issue of stigma will be addressed later in the book.

Samuel is vacuuming the floor. His wife is at work. He's become, at least temporarily, disabled. His doctor has even recommended filing with the government. So, there he is pushing the vacuum cleaner back and forth. His existence feels demeaned and lonely. Instead of ministering in the church, he's now officially a house dad. He is not coping with the new identity very well and there is no one to talk to.

What we have to realize is that we are never truly alone. God is with us. Jesus says to the disciples, *"I will never leave you nor forsake you"* (Heb. 13:5). He departs through the clouds into Heaven. Nevertheless, the Lord dwells within each of us through faith (Ephesians 3:17). So too, must the Holy Spirit (1 John 3:24).

We walk with Him (1 John 1). Talk with Him (1 Thessalonians 5:17). Abide in Him (John 15:5). And, hope in Him (1 Thessalonians 2:19). No, we are definitely not alone. Our dearest Friend is our truest companion. Nevertheless, if we can't bring a friendly world to us, we will go to it.

It is written in Proverbs 18:24, *"A man who has friends must himself be friendly, But there is a friend who sticks closer than a brother."* That closest friend is our Lord. However, can we not ourselves extend friendship? The truth of the matter is depression tempts us to do the opposite of what is socially healthy. Isolation is what the Devil wants. There, we cannot be encouraged or edified by those around us. Isolation beats us down further into a deeper depression. What is better for us is to force ourselves to be out with people. Go to church (cf. Hebrews 10:24-25). Join a social organization. Go to Wal-Mart or a bustling city park and just sit on the bench to watch the people go by. You don't have to say a word.

It is a misnomer among many socialites that there has to be constant talking when two or more people are gathered together. Silence means "the party's dead." Fooey! Couples walking together through the park holding hands, saying nothing, just enjoying the presence of one another maintain some of the most meaningful relationships. The best of friends are able to sit together and not say a word – simply enjoying the company of the other.

Too many ministers make the mistake of being chatterboxes when they are working pastoral care. Hospital visits, for example, should be no longer than the Christian patient needs and no more conversation should be stirred than the patient herself desires. We are not there to shoot the breeze, but to show God's child they are loved and prayed for.

The point is we don't have to be lonely. We do need the fellowshipping interaction of beloved friends and family. Don't lock yourself away in the bedroom. That is a mistake. Contrary to expectation, it actually works in favor of depression to isolate ourselves.

Now, the usual excuse is that we feel too fatigued to be with other people. And, indeed depression does drag us down – but that is a feeling not a true ability of our minds and body. Make the extra effort. Go just one step by getting out of bed. Sit on the couch and watch television with your pet. Step again and reach for the phone. Call a distant relative or someone we haven't spoken with in a long while. Step again and journal your thoughts and feelings onto paper. The goal here is to express and release our emotions, vent. Step again; interact with your children or spouse. Step; go to Wal-Mart with no intention to buy anything, just get out of the house. The thing is, don't think of yourself as having to go from zero to sixty in three seconds flat in getting closer to visiting with friends and loved ones. Take small, intentional steps towards solving your own loneliness issues. Get out of yourself and into the lives of others. Christianity is inherently social. In fact, if we unearth ways to be helpful to others we begin to feel better about ourselves.

VIII.

HARNESSING HALLUCINATIONS
WITH PRAYER DISTRACTIONS

It comes out of nowhere. Blood drips from its fangs. His eyes are rage red. The beast that has chased Samuel since childhood is back from Sheol. Snapping at him with the fierceness of a bangle tiger the beast comes closer and closer. His white fur stained with the victims he's taken alive. Samuel is alone. There is nowhere to run. Nowhere to hide. Like a demon from hell the wolf closes in. He circles around smelling the fear.

Samuel lies there in his bed, in the darkness. It's not a dream. It's real. In his panic he chooses to defend himself. Waving his arms in the air to guard himself from the bites. He kicks but his feet are encumbered with the bed sheets. The white wolf has him penned. The beast comes in for the kill.

"If you don't take your life I will," the wolf says with a voice that whispers with the sound of his dead stepfather.

"Samuel," comes a faint cry. "Samuel! Samuel!" she shouts.

The hallucination vanishes.

Tears flood down Samuel's face as he clings to his supporting wife. She has saved him again.

Distractions

There are psychotic features for some Christians experiencing a manic or mixed episode. Whether visual or audible, hallucinations can be controlled and stopped. Brain chemistry causes them, but like dreams, we can influence their outcome. We can talk back to them. We can rebuke them. We can turn them into something more pleasant. One of the best ways to stop them is to command them to do just that. "In the name of Jesus, Stop!" "In the name of Jesus, Shut-up!" "In the name of Jesus, you are not real!" If you are in the dark, turn on the light. We gain control.

To be sober minded (Titus 2:6) is to think clearly. Hallucinations only seem real. They are not. It is a trick of the mind. Since we know this, we are in the driver's seat.

Psychotropic medications influence brain chemistry such that psychosis can be brought into balance. The spiritual dimension of this issue is (1) do not be afraid of that which is unreal; (2) understand that if an audio hallucination tells us to do something we don't have to obey it – even if it comes from a familiar voice.

If a voice tells us to harm ourselves or somebody else seek immediate psychiatric evaluation. This is evidentiary of an underlying imbalance that must be corrected before we are tempted to follow through with the voice's instructions.

Quoting Scripture

God is always on our side. One of the most powerful weapons we have in our arsenal against the wiles of the Devil is Scripture. Remember, Jesus quotes them when He rebukes the Tempter in Matthew 4. Therefore, it behooves us to memorize as much Bible as we can to use in our favor when we face trickeries.

One of my favorites is Psalm 46:1 *"God is our refuge and strength, A very present help in trouble."* When hallucinations frighten us, we can rebuke them with passages like this. Another is Matthew 11:28 where Jesus says, *"Come to Me, all you who labor and are heavy laden, and I will give you rest."* The goal is to alter what we are focusing on, thinking about. Change our thoughts; change our perceptions. Recite them aloud, repeatedly until the hallucination evaporates.

Prayer

God is concerned with our mind. He wants us stable. Prayer is a most powerful strength the Christian has – that the unbeliever profits little from. Here is a short prayer that we can recite when we hallucinate:

> Dear Heavenly Father,
> You are sovereign,
> I yield my mind to you,
> Run the Devil away.
> In Jesus' name,
> Amen.
>
> Repeat the prayer until the hallucination goes away.

Many Christians must underestimate the full force of prayer because frankly we don't do enough of it. Prayer can heal the sick body and spirit. How do I know that? Because I've seen it done and because the Bible says it is so. *"And the prayer of faith will save the sick, and the Lord will raise him up. And if he has committed sins, he will be forgiven"* (Jas. 5:15). Psychosis is a part of mental illness. Illness. The prayer of faith can heal the illness. Do we believe? Do we have the faith? Are we willing to go down on our face in mighty prayers that will ascend to God's throne room where the Healer sits?

Believers' prayers can stop mania and depression dead in their tracks. Jesus teaches His disciples to pray and He tells them that if their faith is great enough mountains will move (Matthew 6:9ff; 17:20). Oh yes my friend. Believe it.

God is not the author of confusion; Satan is (1 Corinthians 14:33). Therefore, delusions and hallucinations are of the Devil. No. I am not endorsing demonology; I don't believe in that. I am telling you that every disease inflicted on humanity has a spiritual source and that source is sin. Read 1 Corinthians 11:30. In that passage, Christians were abusing communion and consequently fell ill. The human body houses the soul (1 Corinthians 6:19; James 2:26). Thus, what affects the body's chemistry affects the spirit and, what affects the spirit influences the body. The point is God will give us the spiritual fortitude to survive physical and mental trials if we invite Him to.

IX.

SUICIDAL SAINTS

Precious in the sight of the LORD
Is the death of His saints.

Psalm 116:15

We will survive. Don't despair. If you are feeling suicidal right now your best options are (1) call 1-800-SUICIDE in the United States; (2) go to your nearest emergency room; or, (3) dial 911.

In the year 2004 there were 32,439 deaths due to suicide, according to the National Institute of Mental Health (NIH Publication No. 06-4594). The government says this number places suicide as the eleventh leading cause of death in the United States. Of this number many are those suffering with Bipolar Disorder. Many who attempt suicide have been shown to possess decreased levels of serotonin, the chemical we discussed in Chapter III. In truth, that inherently places us at greater risk than the average person to attempt to take our lives. Realize that we are not alone in our thoughts and feelings, or our brain chemistry.

What Our Loved Ones Should Be Watchful For

The following suicide warning signs are from http://www.suicide.org.

- Feeling hopeless
- Expressing hopelessness
- Withdrawing from family and friends
- Sleeping too much or too little
- Feeling tired most of the time
- Gaining or losing a significant amount of weight
- Making statements such as these:
- "I can't go on any longer."
- "I hate this life."
- "There's no point to this stupid life."
- "Everyone would be better of without me."
- "Life is not worth living."
- "Nothing matters anymore."
- "I don't care about anything anymore."
- "I want to die."
- And any mention of suicide
- Writing notes or poems about suicide or death.
- Acting compulsively

- Losing interest in most activities
- Giving away prized possessions
- Writing a will
- No sense of humor
- Facing a perceived "humiliating" situation
- Facing a perceived "failure"
- Feeling excessive guilt or shame
- Acting irrationally
- Being preoccupied with death or dying
- Behaving recklessly
- Irritability
- Frequently complaining about headaches, stomachaches, etc.
- Neglecting personal appearance
- A dramatic change in personal appearance
- A dramatic change in personality
- Performing poorly at work or in school
- Abusing alcohol or drugs
- Inability to concentrate

A large group of these symptoms occur in Major Depressive episodes. Hence, it is smart for loved ones to be on their toes anytime we are ill, and especially while in a mixed state. A mixed bipolar state often gives the impulsivity and energy to follow through with suicidal impulses. It can happen fast.

Spiritual Insight

He is not the God of the dead but of the living (Luke 20:38). God wants us alive. He wants us to thrive. Our Lord says in John 10:10b *"The thief does not come except to steal, and to kill, and to destroy. I have come that they may have life, and that they may have it more abundantly."* Abundant life – that's what God is after.

We have to come to grips with the reality that life is not meant to be easy or pain free. As the apostle Paul has an irritating thorn in his life, so we too must bear our cross. That does not mean we will always be depressed, feel empty, or afflicted in some way. Surely the proverbial old adage is true; suicide is a permanent solution to a temporary problem. There are solutions.

Get down on your knees. Right now. And, pray for God's touch. Experience the Holy Spirit lifting us up. God gives grace to the humble (James 4:6).

To the thief on the cross the Savior says, *"today you will be with Me in Paradise"* (Luke 23:43). We want to go there. How amazing it will be to walk the street of gold (Revelation 21:21). Revelation says that street is like transparent glass. To live in one of God's mansions where Jesus has prepared a place for each of His elect is going to be truly blissful (John 14:1-3). If Jesus came back today, this hour, would we be ready to go Home to be with Him for all eternity? Yes, we say. Suicide is not the way to get there.

It is not for us to decide the day and hour of our departure.

"To everything there is a season, A time for every purpose under heaven: A time to be born, And a time to die; A time to plant, And a time to pluck what is planted; A time to kill, And a time to heal; A time to break down, And a time to build up; A time to weep, And a time to laugh; A time to mourn, And a time to dance; A time to cast away stones, And a time to gather stones; A time to embrace, And a time to refrain from embracing; A time to gain, And a time to lose; A time to keep, And a time to throw away; A time to tear, And a time to sew; A time to keep silence, And a time to speak; A time to love, And a time to hate; A time of war, And a time of peace" (Ecc. 3:1-8).

We will eventually pass away, all of us. When is not left up to us. How is not in our hands. Why is not our decision. Don't let Satan win.

The Devil has been a murderer from the beginning (John 8:44). These feelings we have are our emotions lying to us. Life is worth living. Consider this. Paul writes to the Philippians, *"For to me, to live is Christ, and to die is gain"* (Phil. 1:21). At the time he is in prison, shackled for proclaiming the Good

News. He didn't deserve to be there, anymore than you and I deserve to have a despondent spirit. As the passage continues, Paul tells of the joy he anticipates choosing life over execution. He will be able to spend time with his beloved brethren, who care so deeply for him. He will not be alone in the dungeon anymore. His hope of doing good things for Christ on this side of eternity overpowers his yearning to escape to Heaven's Paradise. It is Satan who wants us to destroy ourselves. Allow Jesus to flush him out of your heart.

It is the general consensus among Christians that suicide is a sin. The logic flows like this. Murder is a sin (Romans 1:29). Therefore, to murder ourselves is sinful. What happens if we die in a sin from which we cannot repent? Read Revelation 21:8. I'm not trying to intimidate or humiliate you, but this is the cold reality faced. And, how serious a matter it is – spiritual life or death. Choose wisely.

It could be argued that God will deal kindly with the mentally ill and that killing oneself in the light of the fact that it is illness that brings one to this brink. But, we just don't know. Paul writes, *"But with me it is a very small thing that I should be judged by you or by a human court. In fact, I do not even judge myself"* (1 Co. 4:3). It could be that saints who commit suicide will see God and live. However, should we test God? Jesus quoted Deuteronomy 6:16 to rebuke the Devil when he tempted Him to commit suicide by throwing Himself off the pinnacle of the temple. Jesus said to him, *"It is written again, 'You shall not tempt the LORD your God'"* (Mat. 4:7). If Jesus can endure such temptations, He can give us strength to do the same. Don't give in. With Christ we will prevail. Hope is our eager expectation.

> *I can do all things through Christ who strengthens me.*
>
> Philippians 4:13

X.

HELP OF THE HOLY SPIRIT

But the Helper, the Holy Spirit, whom the Father will send in My name, He will teach you all things, and bring to your remembrance all things that I said to you.

John 14:26

There's no question about it. We have help, Divine help. Besides the fact that Jesus promised to never forsake us (Hebrews 13:5), is the truth that the Holy Spirit intercedes for us in Heaven. The New Testament plainly says, *"Likewise the Spirit also helps in our weaknesses"* (Rom. 8:26a). Myself, I need all the help I can get!

As we walk in the light with Jesus we sometimes come across shady spots on the path. Its not the good kind of shade like on a cooking hot August afternoon. Its those moments of doubt where we question life and why we have this god-awful disease. We stroll with our Big Brother (Hebrews 2:11) through the garden of grace and we ask childish questions. "Why?"

God sends His Spirit upon us to ease our fears, our anxieties about how we will survive the swings. When we are balanced we wonder when the next trigger will come that sends us up or down. When we are up we lend ourselves to the wild side, but the Holy Spirit helps us remain under control. He protects us from the Savage. Shielding us from going too far. And, when we do slip He lifts us up and brushes our white robes off making us clean once again.

Then one of the elders answered, saying to me, "Who are these arrayed in white robes, and where did they come from?" And I said to him, "Sir, you know." So he said to me, "These are the ones who come out of the great tribulation, and washed their robes and made them white in the blood of the Lamb" (Rev. 7:13-14)

The Holy Spirit sanctifies our souls. That means we are set apart for God's service. We are the world's change agents. Jesus calls us the salt of the earth and lights of the world (Matthew 5:13-14). Like salt, we preserve goodness on the earth. Do you realize that if there were no Christians on the earth, the earth would be spiritually dead? And, if it is dead it is good for nothing but to be condemned, Judged for all eternity. The world is alive because of you. That's how important we are. As lights, we show the world how to come to Jesus – how to find grace and mercy. You, my fellow saint, are one of the world's most important people. The Holy Spirit does that for you.

He guarantees our eternal inheritance. *"In Him you also trusted, after you heard the word of truth, the gospel of your salvation; in whom also, having believed, you were sealed with the Holy Spirit of promise, who is the guarantee of our inheritance until the redemption of the purchased possession, to the praise of His glory"* (Eph. 1:13-14). The Holy Spirit is the living testimony that we belong to God. He is the mark that sets us apart from sinners. The signature of God. Never doubt.

As we writhe with our condition, we must have faith that God is watching over us. He cares. When we come to the point of depression where we can no longer find the words to express our inner feelings, the Holy Spirit understands and petitions the Heavenly Father on our behalf (Romans 8:26). When Satan's afflictions misguide us into doing things we shouldn't the Holy Spirit convicts us (John 16:7-8). He brings us safely back into God's fold.

It is because of the Spirit that we keep going when we feel we can't take another step. "Now hope does not disappoint, because the love of God has been poured out in our hearts by the Holy Spirit who was given to us" (Rom. 5:5). Did we read that right? The Holy Spirit pours out the actual love of God in out hearts. Do we see how much God cares for us? Because the Spirit is in us, God's love dwells in us. Realize this: when we are in a period of normalcy, the Holy Spirit gets the credit for that too. Read Romans

14:17, which speaks of joy in the Holy Spirit. Again in Romans 15:13 we read, *"Now may the God of hope fill you with all joy and peace in believing, that you may abound in hope by the power of the Holy Spirit."*

> *The grace of the Lord Jesus Christ, and the love of God, and the communion of the Holy Spirit be with you all. Amen.*

> 2 Corinthians 13:14

XI.

COPING WITH STIGMA

Blessed are you when they revile and persecute you, and say all kinds of evil against you falsely for My sake. Rejoice and be exceedingly glad, for great is your reward in heaven, for so they persecuted the prophets who were before you.

Matthew 5:11-12

Sometimes good intentions hurt. Samuel is a seasoned Gospel preacher. He knows how to minister to the hurting. His sermons are polished and edifying to all listeners. The brethren at the Denim church love him. The congregation has grown from 75 to 100 members strong in just over a year, largely to his constant evangelistic efforts. Then, it happens.

Samuel, under the stress of financial tensions at home is triggered into bipolar depression. At first, it is moderate and he is able to continue his labor of love. As each day passes, however, he sinks further and further until his depression is severe. Members of the church are beginning to ask questions. "Are you alright, Samuel?"

"I'm just fatigued," he lies.

As Samuel's work slows the concern of his overseers increases. By the time the monthly church leaders' meeting arrives, his pastoral care is at a standstill. His usually excellent sermons are diminishing in quality because of his lack of study and enthusiasm behind the pulpit. The overseers call a special meeting to learn what's going on. They meet one hour before the leaders' meeting.

"What have you been doing with your time?" they ask.

"I've been sick," Samuel replies.

"The sniffles have never affected your work before."

"I'm depressed," Samuel reluctantly confesses.

"We've all been depressed from time to time Samuel. You will be okay. But, you're going to have to pull things together before Vacation Bible School."

"Yes, sir. But, you don't know something. I've been carrying a secret illness that I may have to go into the hospital for if it doesn't improve." Samuel is now shaking as he is about to "let the cat out of the bag." "Brothers, I have Bipolar Disorder."

The overseers took it better than he anticipated. "Samuel, we're your overseers and there should never be secrets of this magnitude between us. How may we help you?"

"I need your prayers and I will go see the doctor." At that, the meeting was concluded. Now comes the leaders' meeting.

It was comprised of the men of the congregation. The church believes men are to be the leaders because the Bible teaches they are the head of their households (1 Corinthians 11:3). It's a principle tradition long held in the Denim church. The meeting ran as meetings due. Financial reports are given and the budget discussed. The grass-mowing schedule is updated as to who will do it and when. Who will orchestrate the order the of worship is decided for the following quarter. Then, as the meeting closes the overseer of the month leads the men in prayer. "And, dear Lord please bless Samuel as he goes to see the doctor about his Bipolar Disorder."

That seemingly harmless and certainly sincere prayer ignited a chain of events that would steal away Samuel's work permanently. Feeling quite down, Samuel leaves as soon as the meeting closes. The men, however, stay and socialize as is their custom. They talk about Samuel and how grateful they are to have him. Then, it begins.

"What is Bipolar Disorder?" Ignorance is the number one cause of stigma.

"My mother has it. It was like hell growing up," one says. This one's mother never took medication. "She would go into these wild rages, smoked crack and had so many men in her bed I lost count." Bad experiences stimulate apprehension.

By the time Samuel gets to the church building Sunday morning the entire congregation has heard about his illness. Some members are comforting, some not. When he stands behind the lectern a sister sitting nearby immediately gets up and moves several pews back. She is heard in a loud whisper, "I can't sit near him. What if he loses it?"

He who holds the purse holds a church. Two rich members of the congregation lost their confidence in Samuel and conspire to get rid of him. They threaten the overseers that they will change churches if they don't cut Samuel loose. With an already weak budget, they cave.

Satan steals the show. He uses everything in his arsenal to stop the productivity of God's workers. If he can convince Christians their minister is tainted in someway, they will lose faith in him. He will have to move on. Stigma is *"something that detracts from the character or reputation of a person, group, etc.; mark of disgrace or reproach"* (Webster's New World Dictionary & Thesaurus). Even their own brethren sometimes persecute fellow Christians living with manic-depressive illness in this way.

The truth of the matter is our condition does not define who we are or what our character is. What is more important is not what other people think of us, but what God thinks. So we have bipolar. So what? Would you tell somebody they are a bad person because they have diabetes? Cancer? We have to educate our fellows.

"My people are destroyed for lack of knowledge," (Hos. 4:6). Ignorance is the first cause of stigma. People frankly don't understand what bipolar illness is or that it is treatable. This breads fear. That which resides in the realm of the unknown is scary to some people and their anxiety turns them judgmental.

People have been fed the myth that all mentally ill people are *crazy*. Motion Pictures feeds this stigma because it sells. *Deranged* people are portrayed as monsters and villains. Again, giving healthy bipolar individuals the same image as those who do not comply with psychiatric treatment.

We do it to ourselves too. If we are in the habit of not taking medicine and we relapse into an episode, especially mania, we taint our own reputation in the eyes of those around us. Too, if we practice immoral behaviors we define ourselves as hypocrites. It is within us to prove to the world that we may lead normal and healthy lives, just as much as the next guy.

Most importantly we accept that we cannot coerce people into changing their opinions. It is uncommon for everybody to like us, whether we are bipolar or not. Don't expect all people, everywhere to like you. They didn't all like Jesus and they won't all like us.

Letting the world into our stigmatized world is not always bad. We're not all public figures like Samuel and not all of God's churches are like Denim. Being open about having bipolar allows us the freedom to gain edifying love and support from others. We can educate them. We can set the example of being a genuinely Christ-like person who is battling a brain disease. Opening up gives others the opportunity to support us when we are down and patiently treat us with kindness while manic. In truth, stigma will not end until the majority of us take a stand, band together and show Satan who really runs the show.

The choice is liberating. We no longer have to hide. After all, *"A friend loves at all times"* (Proverbs 17:17a).

XII.

HEALING WITH JESUS

So He came to Nazareth, where He had been brought up. And as His custom was, He went into the synagogue on the Sabbath day, and stood up to read. And He was handed the book of the prophet Isaiah. And when He had opened the book, He found the place where it was written: "The Spirit of the LORD is upon Me, Because He has anointed Me To preach the gospel to the poor; He has sent Me to heal the brokenhearted, To proclaim liberty to the captives And recovery of sight to the blind, To set at liberty those who are oppressed; To proclaim the acceptable year of the LORD." Then He closed the book, and gave it back to the attendant and sat down. And the eyes of all who were in the synagogue were fixed on Him. And He began to say to them, "Today this Scripture is fulfilled in your hearing."

Luke 4:16-21

We are survivors. Undoubtedly, Satan has afflicted us with a horrible disease. Bipolar Disorder is not for the fainthearted. It is not from the illness itself that we seek healing, though that would be a great blessing –

and certainly it is not beyond the power of God. Odds are, however, we will struggle with this ailment for the remainder of our lives. We, like the apostle Paul have a thorn. *"And He said to me, 'My grace is sufficient for you, for My strength is made perfect in weakness.' Therefore most gladly I will rather boast in my infirmities, that the power of Christ may rest upon me"* (2 Co. 12:9). That all-sufficient grace is where we rest in our weakness.

Jesus has experienced emotional upheaval (Matthew 27:46; John 11:35). He understands our suffering. We go to Him for consoling and He is there. The soothing mercy comes when we need it most. *"Come to Me, all you who labor and are heavy laden, and I will give you rest"* (Mat. 11:28). The same temptations we experience, He has known too. *"For we do not have a High Priest who cannot sympathize with our weaknesses, but was in all points tempted as we are, yet without sin"* (Heb. 4:15).

We must trust Jesus. Taking our spirit by the hand He leads us through the valley of fear and doubt. Lifting our heart to Heaven's highest level, our High Priest intercedes with the Father of mercies and God of all comfort (2 Corinthians 1:3). Reigning in our hearts He has truly become the Lord of our life. We have faith in Him because He has faith in us.

Jesus is our best Friend. He loves us like an older Brother sheltering a little sister (Hebrews 2:11). Actually, as a member of the Lord's church we are married to Him. She is His virgin bride (Revelation 21:2). He cares for us with unconditional love and unmerited favor. Think of the sacrifice. *"For the death that He died, He died to sin once for all; but the life that He lives, He lives to God"* (Rom. 6:10).

In Christ, we have become living sacrifices (Romans 12:1). Every good thing we do or even think glorifies the One who has set us free. We are living letters bearing testimony to the healing in our souls (2 Corinthians 3:2). Everywhere we go, sick or not, we impart light to the dark world (Philippians 2:15). Jesus is alive in us (John 15:4). Inasmuch as we allow Him to work through us, Christians living with bipolar may become one of the most potent forces for Good on earth.

> *The people who sat in darkness have seen a great light,*
>
> *And upon those who sat in the region and shadow of death Light has dawned.*
>
> Matthew 4:16

BIBLIOGRAPHY

National Institute of Mental Health. http://www.nimh.
nih.gov

Suicide.org http://www.suicide.org

Holy Bible, New King James Version (Thomas Nelson,
Inc., 1982).

ABOUT THE AUTHOR

Donny Weimar has worked with many people with mental illnesses. He has Bipolar Disorder and fights to win over stigma. Donny has a wife and three children. His wife is an accomplished vocal musician.

Donny has worked as a Gospel Preacher for more than twenty years. His children are brilliant, making straight A's. The youngest has skipped ahead one grade. All of them are avid readers.

Made in the USA
Middletown, DE
06 March 2017